PERSONAL GROWTH

PERSONAL GROWTH

PEBBLES HOPKE

PALMETTO
PUBLISHING
Charleston, SC
www.PalmettoPublishing.com

Copyright © 2024 by Pebbles Hopke

All rights reserved.

No portion of this book may be reproduced, stored in a retrieval system, or transmitted in any form by any means-electronic, mechanical, photocopy, recording, or other–except for brief quotations in printed reviews, without prior permission of the author.

Paperback ISBN: 979-8-8229-3868-7

TABLE OF CONTENTS

Chapter 1　Is Spiritual, between You and God ······1
Chapter 2　Is Disciplined ······················ 8
Chapter 3　Patience with Self and Others ········ 16
Chapter 4　Changed Behavior ·················· 22
Chapter 5　Changed Attitude ·················· 30
Chapter 6　Different for Everyone ··············· 36
Chapter 7　Sometimes Mandatory ·············· 45
Chapter 8　Takes Encouragement ·············· 49

CHAPTER 1
IS SPIRITUAL, BETWEEN YOU AND GOD

What is the first thing you do when you wake up? Drink that hot cup of coffee, Frappuccino, or latte with foam? Take a quick or long hit of that vape, cigarette, or cannabis? Take a sip or down that cold brewski? Do a quick line to wake up or take another hit because your body physically depends on that drug? Do you turn to your loved one and greet them for the day or pray? Do you pry and pry your kids out of bed with bribes and kisses to prepare them for the school day? Your core values and beliefs you think will define you—and maybe so, yet we should let and allow God, the good Lord to define who we are, individually.

Are you a wife, husband, father, mother, CEO, teacher, military, nurse, hairstylist, nail technician, or the president of the United States? We all have a job that needs to be done. We all have things that are required of us to do. Do you have certain obligations? Are you obligated as parents by being responsible? Are you obligated to do chores for your parents or yourself if you want a clean room and house? Are there people that are expectant of you and from you? What do you expect of and from yourself?

Do not let what you do, or your unhealthy habits define who you are—that is not you, it is a something that you can break, with help of course, because believe it or not, "we all need help." A dear friend said this to me once when I was probably too afraid to ask for it, not knowing at the time I was letting pride get to me. God says, 'So we say with confidence, "The Lord is my helper; I will not be afraid. What can mere mortals do to me?" (Hebrews 13:6 NIV)

Are you thirsty for his words? Feed yourself the word, God's word—pray and then read the Bible. You will feel replenished and full of the Holy Spirit. Drink a cold glass of water, adding lemon to help cleanse and detox your insides. Eat a healthy meal and breakfast. My dad always used to tell me, "Mi hita, make sure your man eats good, especially in the morning. He's got to eat like a king in the morning and a prince in the evening." If we have the proper nutrients each of our bodies requires and needs, what we eat—besides God's word—will fuel us, giving us energy and God's strength in order to accomplish all that he has planned for us. Jeremiah 29:11 NIV states: "For I know the plans

I have for you," declares the LORD, "plans to prosper you and not to harm you, plans to give you hope and a future." Now that is reassuring. Do you ever feel empty inside? Do you ever wonder why you are here on this earth and what your purpose is? The Bible says in Romans 8:28 (NIV): "And we know that in all things God works for the good of those who love him, who have been called according to his purpose." Proverbs 19:21 says, "Many are the plans in a person's heart, but it is the LORD'S purpose that prevails." At times we may think that the plans we have made will work out just how we want, and then something happens in our lives to change them. God has better plans for us, if our plans do not work out according to what we think should or shouldn't happen. Ephesians 2:10 says, "For we are God's handiwork, created in Christ Jesus to do good works, which God prepared in advance for us to do." We all have purpose and meaning, we just need to find that hidden purpose and meaning.

It says in Hebrews 13:16: "And do not forget to do good and to share with others, for with such sacrifices God is pleased." Practice generosity and never hurt anyone, sharing freely what God has given you. 1 Peter 4:9 states, "Offer hospitality to one another without grumbling."

Once you come to know Christ, he fills all the voids you ever turned to, thought you needed and or wanted externally. You will realize that one person can't fulfill all of our needs, not all the time but God can—this is why we need God. Not all the drugs in the world will fill that void you feel. All the alcohol you can consume would not be enough—you would still feel sad, empty, or lost inside. No amount of money could truly satisfy the human mind or heart, except for the one and only Jesus Christ himself. Hebrews 13:5 says, "Keep your lives free from the love of money and be content with what you have, because God has said, "Never will I leave you; never will I forsake you." He is that void; he fills all voids.

No matter what you go through, personally, and professionally God sees all the difficulties and hard work you are putting in and going through alone and while at work. Do not worry or be concerned with performance. Continue to please the Lord if you believe and have a personal relationship with him. If you do not know who the good Lord is just yet, do not worry or have cause for concern—God looks out for everyone, the good, the bad, the believers and non-believers.

Your day or morning could look and be completely different than that of your neighbors. As long as you are one step closer to where you want to be in life, and for that day, you are well on your way to becoming successful. Do not compare all you have done so far with what you have not yet accomplished.

It all boils down to your choices—good and bad, to the minute choices, right down to the terrible life changing choices, the ones we cannot come back from. The choices that we have no choice but to live with for the rest of our lives. The Lord gives freedom in choices. 2 Corinthians 3:17 states, "Now the Lord is the Spirit, and where the Spirit of the Lord is, there is freedom." And in John 8:36: "So if the son sets you free, you will be free indeed." Free from sin; free from bondage; free from whatever it is that is holding you back from God's glory and his good.

Galatians 5:13-4 says, "You, my brothers and sisters, were called to be free. But do not use your freedom to indulge the flesh; rather, serve one another humbly in love. For the entire law is fulfilled in keeping this one command: "Love your neighbor as yourself." Even though we have the freedom to choose, we must choose wisely in our everyday choices. Just because no one can see what it is, you might choose to do behind closed doors, that you wouldn't necessarily do in front of people in fear of the right judgement being placed upon you, because what you are choosing is not good for you, your health, behavior, mentality, physical and or spiritual self, still choose to do right. 1 Peter 2:16 reminds us to, "Live as free people, but do not use your freedom as a cover-up for evil; live as God's slaves." Living in obedience to the Lord.

Once your relationship with Jesus starts to grow closer, you will notice a difference in your surroundings. You will notice the way you perceive things differently than before and possibly have a new view of how you see the world and the people in it. You will have a new vison that God brings to your life for you to see, new plans that are different from before you came to know Christ.

    Some things are better left unsaid and some things are better left between you and God! He knows your heart. What is not said or prayed aloud will surely be heard from your heart—no words need to be spoken during those times when you cannot speak what is on your mind. Maybe you feel too angry, hurt, sad, or broken to speak to the Lord. When you feel distracted and or when you are alone and still do not have it in you to say the things that are on your heart and mind, don't worry—know that God still hears you and he sees the real you. The one you are too afraid to let anyone else see. He loves you regardless.

    Sometimes you can make plans and then either you screw them up or God has other amazing plans that are beyond comprehension. Proverbs 16:9 says, "In their hearts humans plan their course, but the LORD establishes their steps." All humans have value, purpose, and something to add to this world, more importantly to add to GOD'S kingdom. When trusting in Gods plans for your life, you let go of the ability to try and be in control of everything and or the outcome of things and situations in life. God is in control. Psalm 115:3 says, "Our God is in heaven; he does whatever pleases him."

    The connection you feel with Jesus Christ, once you come to know him personally, through choice and

PERSONAL GROWTH

willingness, will help you listen to his word and advice on life through scripture. Still choosing, as hard as it may be sometimes to obey his word, by the things we do daily. How we choose to live our lives and reflecting all that Jesus Christ himself is, will benefit us in more ways than one.

When you choose to follow Christ, the beginning is bittersweet, like a fruit that isn't quite ripe yet. At times you might feel like you're physically, mentally, and possibly even spiritually dying. Once ripened, the fruit-of-your Spirit-will be sweeter than the next fruit. What this means is that Christ is giving you time to grow and mature in his Spirit. The old you is ready to leave, ready and willing to embrace the new and improved you.

When you pray with good intentions for anything with belief and hopes of having or gaining what it is you really want, trust and believe it can and will be yours in God's perfect timing. Of course, you have to do your part consistently by being willing and ready to do the work of the Lord. Whoever it is you are really working for, yourself, the enemy, your friends, co-workers, your boss, your family, spouse, children, etcetera, will show outwardly in the lives around you. Your fruits will eventually show, starting inward then eventually everyone around you will see what God is and has been doing in your life.

CHAPTER 2
IS DISCIPLINED

Discipline takes challenging work and consistency. Staying the course, even when it gets hard—trust and believe that there will be times when it gets hard. There will be times when you want to give up, and when you do, to put it simply, don't. Giving up is not trying at all. You have to keep trying, no matter what. What is it that pushes you and drives you to do what you do in the first place, good or bad?

You choose to do your duties whether you want to or not, whether you feel like it or not. Colossians 3:22 says, "Slaves, obey your earthly masters, in everything; and do it, not only when their eye is on you and to curry their favor, but with sincerity of heart and reverence for the Lord." A person's job needed and still needs to be done. Some of us have been called to do things such as household chores and duties, even when we do not feel like it.

Persistent hard work pays off, and your reward will be great. Colossians 3:23-24 says, "Whatever you do, work at it with all your heart, as working for the Lord, not for human masters, since you know that you will receive an inheritance from the Lord as a reward." Of course, we will have our eternal salvation. John 3:16 says, "For God so loved the world that he gave his one and only son, that whoever believes in him shall not perish but have eternal life." There is more to our future that we do not know that the good Lord has set aside, planned, and prepared for us—a place of righteousness. Mathew 6:33 says, "But seek first his kingdom and his righteousness, and all these things will be given to you as well." Seek peace and you will have peace Gods peace, seek patience, kindness, understanding, and compassion, and you will have all these things and then some.

Every individual has their own purpose and calling for their lives—whether it be good or bad, you serve a purpose. Figuring out that purpose takes time, and with God's help you can and eventually will. When you do, do not run from the calling God has on your life—everything in it will be used for his purpose and his mighty goodwill. In Isaiah 46:10 the Lord states: "I make known the end from the beginning, from ancient times, what is still to come." I say, 'My purpose will stand, and I will do all that I please.'

Personal growth takes enough discipline to have self-control. "It teaches us to say 'No' to ungodliness and worldly passions, and to live self-controlled, upright and godly lives in this present age." (Titus 2:12 NIV). Do not be afraid of physical, mental, or emotional pain. 2 Timothy 1:7 reminds us, "For the Spirit God gave us does not make us timid, but gives us power, love and self-discipline." Do not be afraid of being soberminded and feeling what is naturally normal. 1 Peter 4:7 says, "The end of all things is near. Therefore, be alert and of sober mind so that you may pray." When our mind is gone, lost, or warped by the lies of the enemy or because of certain choices to use and abuse drugs, or substances-our minds can and do get clouded and therefore are free from a clear conscious in order to think clearly for ourselves or yourself.

Learning to control your temper and anger is important. James 1:19-20 states: "My dear brothers and sisters, take note of this: Everyone should be quick to listen, slow to speak and slow to become angry, because human anger does not produce the righteousness that God desires." There is a difference between an angry person and a person who gets angry momentarily or temporarily. Perhaps, but does not sin in and out of anger. For the Lord says it is okay to be angry, but it is not okay to sin in your anger. A person who gets angry often could be considered hot-tempered. It says in Ephesians 4:26: "In your anger do not sin:" Do not let the sun go down while you are still angry, and do not give the devil a foothold." Try to captivate your thoughts before you act on something evil and do something that is not good for you, your health or will bring harm to yourself or others.

Having control of your tongue is crucial. 1 Peter 3:10 says, "For, 'whoever would love life and see good days must keep their tongue from evil and their lips from deceitful speech." Controlling your tongue—knowing when and when not to speak up—can and will save you from saying the wrong things to someone you love. "There is a time and place for everything," my father used to say to me. Ecclesiastes 3:1 says, "There is a time for everything, and a season for every activity under the heavens," meaning if now is not the time and place to say or do something in that moment, then you probably shouldn't. If the urge and desire is strong enough in your heart, mind, and soul, telling you to keep quiet or on the hush-hush, then I would suggest keeping and staying quiet. For however long God is asking you too. If you also get a little nudge from the Holy Spirit pushing you to speak up or do something in those moments, I suggest you listen to that pull.

Harvesting what you sow will lead to reaping the benefits when you do not give up. When you put forth effort, God gets credit for the rewards—you choose what you sow. Galatians 6:9 says, "Let us not become weary in doing good, for at the proper time we will reap a harvest if we do not give up." So, do not give up on the people in your life; do not give up on that project you have been working on for what seems like forever. Do not give up on that loan, waiting to be approved.

Do not give up on your workout or exercise routine. Keep working on that school paper. Don't give up on nurses, our military men and women, your teachers, leaders and or President etcetera. we all have a role and play a purpose.

Repeat, doing the same thing to maintain or achieve the same goal; do this differently to get a different result. Doing the dishes every day or after every meal will result in clean dishes—this is a habitual act. Even when we do not want to do the dishes or other chores that require our attention, doing them regardless will be the only way we have anything clean to eat off. We might not think about doing the dishes, but we know that they are in the sink or on the counter waiting to be done.

Routine is built from determination. When you follow through with wherever God has you in your life, he will not leave you hanging. In Philippians 1:6, it says, "being confident of this, that he who began a good work in you will carry it on to completion until the day of Christ Jesus." Follow through with what you say you are going to do, and if it is hard to keep your word, then do not say anything at all—go about your business quietly. No one but God needs to know the good you are doing in secret. You will be rewarded openly for all the good you do secretly in God's own way and timing.

We might grope and moan, but the good Lord says in Philippians 2:14 to "do everything without grumbling or arguing." John 6:43 says, "Stop grumbling among yourselves," Jesus answered." We may at times grumble, mumble, stutter, or stammer under our breath, yet when asked to do something, do it and get it done without hasty negative words or actions. The results will be way more delightful.

You're asked, "Do you want to work out with me?" You reply, "No thank you—it seems like work." Interesting that the word "work" is in there—maybe you would rather exercise because it sounds better. Do what works for you and your physical body. Repeat your workout regimen to get the desired results you are looking for in your physical health.

Setting and using multiple alarms for different things, such as activities, appointments, and events are minor reminders of the significant and meaningful events happening in your life, even if you do not see it or understand the significance.

Setting unrealistic goals for yourself will only end up in failure and a major letdown. Do not—I repeat, do not—tell yourself you can do something if you know it is out of your reach, authority and control. Meaning if you cannot help yourself or others in the process of being disciplined, that of the Lords, discipline to achieve what is good, do not make unrealistic goals—make them achievable. In Proverbs 3:11-12 says, "My son, do not despise the LORD'S discipline, and do not resent his rebuke, because the LORD disciplines those he loves, as a father the son he delights in." Attaining your personal accomplishments will not only feel exhilarating, but achieving these specific goals step by step will benefit yourself in more ways than one. Benefiting Mentally, emotionally, physically, and hopefully spiritually, if nothing else. Making your personal set goals attainable, by the way you approach what it is you are doing, with care and ease.

Choosing to do something even when you do not want to is discipline. Making the right decisions for yourself now, will benefit you in the long run. In the words of the great Abraham Lincoln: "Discipline is choosing between what you want now and what you want most." Is what you want most, going to cost you? Is what you want most too hard to achieve? Is what you want unattainable? Or is what you want now worth it? Is what you want now worth what you may lose later in life?

As humans we want instantaneous results (some of the things we wish we had, we want right now, to come easy, to not have to work hard for what it is we are after). To feel that high immediately, to wait or not to wait, to take that next dose, or to not feel anything. What would we give just to not feel anything or be overwhelmed with thoughts, feelings, and emotions?

Acting on impulse based on current emotion, future worry, doubt, and or fear, without thinking through the consequences, could lead to possible regrets. Over time, discipline gets easier because you are practiced in what it is you are training yourself to do. The more you think about why you are disciplining yourself, the better it gets with time. Discipline never feels good, but, in the end, you will be thankful you had it. Discipline can be painful but is needed in order to grow and learn from our past behaviors, which have not served us well.

    Flowers grow and bloom, taking their time. In the same sense, it takes a person to grow and mature in their physical and spiritual body. It does not matter the length of time for growth and beauty to fully come to fruition. In the same way plants need to be watered, our spirits need to be watered with the Lord's refreshing word. Humans are like flowers in the sense that each of us grow and change with time, and over time we will witness the beauty that comes with it. Giving yourself the amount of time you need to be able to grow wiser, in God's word and in the Spirit. Time makes us wiser in your decision-making. Remember to water yourself with things that are good and godly.

    With anything that is bad for you, it is better not to want anything that is no good for you, especially drugs or any immediate satisfaction and gratifications, for the Lord is the ultimate satisfaction. You have the discipline and ability to overcome any obstacles that may come your way. When you do not feel like doing what is good for you, do it anyway-that my friends is discipline.

CHAPTER 3
PATIENCE WITH SELF AND OTHERS

It takes time Being patient in affliction with others during demanding times. When it is the hardest to be patient with someone, try anyways and see where it gets you. Romans 12:12 says, "Be joyful in hope, patient in afflictions, faithful in prayer." When you are being patient with yourself and others around you, you are in service to the Lord. The one that shows patience is teaching others to be patient, as well. With this, God's patience is then passed on to the next person in hopes they will pass it on to the next, showing who God is. So, ladies and gentlemen, you have learned God's patience and therefore are like Christ, Christ like. Does this make you rejoice in his goodness?

Waiting in line at a coffee shop and in a rush, a businessman shouted angrily, "Sheesh, what's taking

PERSONAL GROWTH

so long?" A soft-spoken and reassuring voice came from behind the counter. "Sir, there are still people ahead of you that we need to serve before we can get to you." The businessman was impatient, annoyed, and irritable. "Well it doesn't take that long to brew up some coffee, for Chrissake!" He exclaimed. Other customers waiting patiently in line minded their own business, while others rolled their eyes. The person in front of the businessman was not in a hurry, so he gestured the businessman to move ahead of him in line. The businessman was still scuffled that he had to wait at all. He felt entitled. He sighed and puffed, as he still had to wait like everyone else. The person now in front of the businessman allowed him to cut in front of him, as well. The businessman was somewhat surprised at this, that two people would allow him to go in front of them. One more ahead, the coffee worker finally got to the businessman's order. When he was done ordering, he said "How much will it be?" The worker behind the counter said, "Don't worry about it, the gentleman before you paid for your items." The businessman was astonished. He received not only grace, but generosity at its finest. He experienced multiple people being kind to him—maybe God knew he needed that kindness and generosity, so maybe one day he can repay someone else with the same. "What an impatient person," one customer thought to herself, baffled after he had left in a hurry. Someone had to show God's patience with this person in order for him, the impatient person, to learn patience—it was an opportunity for them to see who God is and may have been the start of him getting to know Christ for who he is. God is patient. Sometimes the Lord is kind to us even when we do not deserve it—continue being kind anyway.

Being patient with yourself, knowing that you will have to start over, maybe even several times, before getting it right. What's right, you may ask? What it is you are trying to make right if you want to make anything right at all. What needs to be right with yourself, or right with the relationships in your life? Do you want to see changes? Do you want to see growth? Do you want to see different results? The work for these different results needs to be done in order to see that growth and change. Over time with the right amount of work put in, you will definitely see good results. During these challenging times, you will notice slight changes, in your thoughts and behavior. Soon it will not be a problem for you to overcome little challenges you have to face. It will not be problematic when you have to wait on someone in line at the coffee shop next time you are in a rush to get to work. Next time leave your house ten minutes earlier, so you know you will have time to stop at the gas station to get snacks and still be called punctual when you arrive at work, instead of the employee who is always ten minutes late.

Understanding patience takes practice. I do not think anyone has patience right away coming out of the womb. We must wait on our mothers, fathers, or caretakers when we are infants, waiting on them to change our diapers, feed us, burp us, hold us, comfort us, and love us. As we age and become toddlers, we patiently wait for our parents to prepare and cook our meals for us. As toddlers, young children, teenagers, and into adulthood, we still continue to wait on each other. If we are not first patient with ourselves, then how can we expect to be patient with others? While waiting for someone else to cook our food, it could mean waiting in line at the drive-through Taco Bell or inside Wendy's; it could mean waiting in the living room while watching your favorite TV program, or at the dining room table while your spouse hooks up a *delectable* dish they saw on Pinterest. Either way we are waiting, practicing patience and serving each other during this process. One thing of many to mention; humanity as one kind must wait on, is meal preparation and cooking even if someone else or ourselves is doing it.

You cannot serve love with hate in your heart, for if hate belongs in your heart, how can you have love? The opposite of hate is love. In Proverbs 10:12 says, "Hatred stirs up conflict, but love covers all wrongs." God is love; love is God. 1 John 4:8 says, "Whoever does not love does not know God, because God is love." Something Mi Tu papa used to tell me, and one of the first things I ever learned about God, is that he is love. Whatever you do, do it out of love, not out of motivation for self or evil intentions. 1 Peter 4:8 says, "Above all, love each other deeply, because love covers over a multitude of sins."

In line at the restroom, a mother says, "Wait your turn." Her child responds, "Mommy, I really have to go!" The mother states, "I know—I understand, sweetheart, but you're going to have to hold it a little longer." Trying to explain to your child at an age where they may not understand that sometimes we do not have a choice but to wait can be overwhelming. There are times we must wait on other people before we can do what it is we need or have to do. Reminding ourselves to wait patiently in the same manner we may have to remind our own children sometimes is helpful; it helps us remember that you are not the only one waiting.

To be patient, we must learn to wait, with no attitude, complaining, groaning, or moaning. James 5:9 says, "Don't grumble against one another, brothers and sisters, or you will be judged. The judge is standing at the door." Stop all the nagging, bickering, and yapping between each other, the Lord says. It probably looks ridiculous to him when his children are not getting along well. It brings joy to the Lord when his children do get along.

Do not abuse the Lord's kindness, patience, and mercy once you come to know his true grace. 2 Peter 3:9 says, "The Lord is not slow in keeping his promise, as some understand slowness. Instead he is patient with you, not wanting anyone to perish, but everyone to come to repentance." Once you discover who God really is, you will want everyone to come to know Christ in order to fulfill his purposes.

God is more than patient when it comes to him waiting on us to turn away from our own selfish ways. He waits on us and he wants us to wait on him. If we are going to make the conscious decision to wait on the Lord, let us do it joyfully and productively. Titus 3:14 claims: "Our people must learn to devote themselves to doing what is good, in order to provide for urgent needs and not live unproductive lives."

CHAPTER 4
CHANGED BEHAVIOR

Changing behavior takes dedication in many forms—your time, energy, and efforts to the things, people, and places that matter most. Making the right decision—which may be hard to make, regardless of how you may feel—will benefit you further in the long run than if you chose a wrong decision. Recognizing possible addictions from not using, like porn, sex, gambling, money, fame, power, food, or gluttony, is the first step in making change. Proverbs 23:2 says, "and put a knife to your throat if you are given to gluttony." Realizing you have a problem will help you want to make a change.

Kicking old unpleasant habits in the butt and changing any behavior that is and or was harmful to oneself and others. Resisting temptation. You can do this by using and preaching God's word. Praying is also very important. James 4:7 says, "Submit yourselves, then, to God. Resist the devil, and he will flee from you."

A prayer I like to pray myself is this: "I rebuke the devil, In Jesus name, Amen." Seek to be dedicated to pleasing the Lord in all we say and do, in thoughts, deeds, and actions. A person will show and prove through their actions that they are no longer doing what was not good for them or to those close to them, family, or friends. The things we do out of habit could be what we become, even if we don't intentionally mean to become what could possibly destroy us in the end. If we do not stop, assess, evaluate, reflect, and become self-aware of our everyday choices, down to what we eat, could affect each individual differently. So, let's make a good habit of becoming all the good things to better ourselves and our lives for the greater good of God's Kingdom, for your future, my future and the future of all those willing to partake in The Lords' work and his word. The Lord has many works, wonders, and miracles he has done, is yet to do and will do in his timing.

Changed behavior means doing something different than you did the day before. Changing your ways leads to you becoming better than you were yesterday, and coming farther than you were last week. Changing behavior from sin will be a daily fight and battle, but the battle does not have to be yours. All battles are for the Lord—give your burdens, struggles, and worries to him. Perhaps you might be standing and or sitting in your own way, fighting battles against yourself. Get up, get moving, and get going. Even if it hurts, the gains will be worth it. The mental, emotional, and spiritual pain will hurt when you decide to change for the better. The healing process, too, will be totally worth it when and once you have reached your healing.

Everyone makes mistakes, whether we know they do or not. Only God knows and can see what goes on behind closed doors, when we think no one is looking. Learning from those mistakes and not making them again will prevent heartache and much trouble, if we choose not to make the same mistake that caused heartache and turmoil in the first place. When we make a mistake or slip up, most of the time no one plans too. Okay, so you slipped up—once you give yourself enough time to get over your little ordeal, it's time to move on. Leave that slip up in the past and move forward with your life if you so choose. If you aren't ready to move on or forward with your life, then that is okay, too—staying right where you are at is probably where God wants you to be. If you are in a position, situation, or certain circumstances, sometimes we cannot leave or move on because God is trying to mold us into who he wants us to be in that very moment to discover who he is—who he is in us and who we are in him.

Your unhealthy habits, rather, will be dust in the wind when you decide to do better by choosing to make wiser decisions, in those moments when you are being tempted and or ready to make a decision that you will later regret. When you do decide to do something different for a change, at first you may think, "I can't do this." Rest assured that you can—you will get through the toughest parts of your struggle, probably when no one is looking.

Quitting cold turkey, making that change, that difference, that will make the ultimate difference in your life because of that change, from those simple choices that you chose and choose to make—more importantly the wise choices, the hard but right choices in God's eyes that you have to make, as hard as it is, by doing or deciding to quit overtime, weaning off of whatever drug it is you are trying to free yourself from. If you are trying to quit for reasons other than God, like yourself in order to better your health, or your relationships, that is okay too. Either way, the decision and choice to quit the bad habit in the first place is an exceptionally good start.

In place of smoking and or choosing a bad habit, replace it with something healthy and productive, like going for a brisk walk or jog, to clear your head. Praying and asking the good Lord to help you resist the temptation you are fighting is also important. There is no need to fight—let the battle be the Lord's responsibility. He will give you the desire to make the best decision, helping you become wiser in that moment of temptation. There is always room for escape—God will help you get out of certain situations. In 1 Corinthians 10:13, it says, "No temptation has overtaken you except what is common to mankind. And God is faithful;

he will not let you be tempted beyond what you can bear. But when you are tempted, he will also provide a way out so that you can endure it." God will not give you more than you can manage. When it comes to the devil and his attempts to tempt us with his evil desires, wants, and lies, his goal is to keep you depressed and down in the dumps. He wants you to stay in doubt. His attempts are to get you to stay in and live in the flesh, not the spirit. Only God gives us spirit of self-control and discipline. God gave us the fruit of the spirit, which is good, meek and kind. Galatians 5:22-23 says, "But the fruit of the Spirit is love, joy, peace, forbearance, kindness, goodness, faithfulness, gentleness and self-control. Against such things there is no law." God reassures you and comforts you in times of need and desperation.

Choosing to use in order to avoid either your own feelings, or avoid someone else and what they put us through. Soon what you want, you won't anymore, you will be disgusted with yourself. You yourself will want to change. Are you or have you purposely avoided getting things, done like household chores? I have put them off or waited to get certain things done in the past based off temporary feelings and emotions.

Procrastinating—waiting until the last minute to do something—will only delay and put off the good work the Lord is trying to do in you. Although he is very much still at work with what he is doing in each of our lives, we just cannot always see all the clever work it is that

God is or may be doing. We put things off to avoid either confrontation, avoid life, avoid resolution, avoid conflict that could be resolved when and if talked about, with understanding like the Lord. Having patience with an open and listening ear, like Jesus. I have done this a lot in the past, avoid my feelings by trying to hide them under a rug and mask them until I've learned that some things do not need my immediate attention while other important things in my life—like God and my family—take priority. Everything else takes a back seat, but they are still there in my life for me to protect through the power of prayer. When God puts a person, situation, worry, or thought that won't go away on your mind, then it is imperative to stop what you are doing, ruin everything that satan may be doing, and pray for that person, situation, worry or thought that is on your mind, in that moment in time. I promise you will have immediate peace when you talk to the Lord—and if you aren't satisfied, then keep talking to the Lord until you are. The thing about it is, you will never be satisfied with just one prayer. Once God answers your prayers, it can become addicting to want to talk to him more on the daily, as well as living for him and not for yourself. It is challenging to stay on the straight and narrow path, but is it is possible—with God, all things are possible. Even though you might temporarily be satisfied with worldly things the enemy offers, it will never compare to being satisfied with what the Lord has to offer.

Overdoing it is something many humans tend to do from time to time, whether they mean to or not. Learning not to overdo it is key to having enough self-control to say no. Sometimes, though, when you are in the moment it is impossible to say no.

Wasting time is another reason for drug use and abuse—waiting for time to pass us by while our minds are temporarily out of this world or in another dimension. How can we do what God has called us to do if we are not in our right state of mind, in order to do what we need or want to do with a clear concise. If you are bored, embrace it. Being bored from time to time is not always a dreadful thing. Learn to be bored—new ideas can come to mind if you let them, or you can choose to ignore them. Choosing which bright ideas to bring to life will be the decision maker—your ideas are your own. Whatever you produce, go with it—who cares if no one else likes your idea! Your bright idea could be a million, a billion, no trillion-dollar idea—you never know.

Thinking back to routine discussed in chapter two, what behaviors or choices are leading you to do the same thing repeatedly that are just no good for you? Your ways will change when you realize you no longer want what's not good for you. Of course, it takes time to get to where you need and want to be—that better place in your life— but that time will be beneficial in the long run.

Move forward; don't look back unless it is to reflect on all the good you have done for the Lord and his glory. Never stop to look in the rearview unless you're stopping to look back on the reflections in your life and how far you've come. If you are going to act, act on behalf of God. Be who you were meant to be. Take action on your part and do something about the change that you so desperately want to see. If you are going to change, change for the better; if you are going to grow, grow in Christ.

If you want to change and are taking the necessary steps in order to do so, and if you are tired while doing it, then by all means do it tired. If you are sore from your exercise routine, then continue while sore. It is hard right now, but it will get easier with practice. Change, grow, make different choices.

CHAPTER 5
CHANGED ATTITUDE

Mindset is everything, taking every thought captive. The good Lord says in 2 Corinthians 10:5: "We demolish arguments and every pretension that sets itself up against the knowledge of God, and we take captive every thought to make it obedient to Christ." Change your attitude when necessary, and ask yourself "What can I do differently that will change my results?" Take your thoughts captive by not acting on any impure thoughts or sins. A changed attitude will show in a person's perspective through the way that they act and behave. Colossians 3:10 says, "and have put on the new self, which is being renewed in knowledge in the image of its creator."

Thinking differently than before can lead to having a changed mind and heart. Romans 12:12 says, "Let God transform you into a new person by changing the way you think." 1 Corinthians 13:11 says, "When I was a child, I talked like a child, I thought like a child. When

PERSONAL GROWTH

I became a man, I put the ways of childhood behind me." Now as an adult, I put away childish things as part of maturing. Looking back and reflecting on your old ways and instead think of new ways the Lord has shown you through people and the Bible, in your everyday life and experiences. Something my father said in one of his dearest letters to me was this: "Also remember information, however well absorbed, is worthless without applying that which is learned." This came from the Lord, Thursday, April 19th, 2012, as he put these words in my father's heart, and in his mind to write me from prison for me to share with the world.

Anything we choose to absorb, take in, learn, or understand does not mean anything unless we effectively put it to good use, like GODS' word as a minor example. So, what we learn from God's word through reading the Bible is his instruction. Read any version or translation you choose that you are comfortable with. The version I personally like and enjoy and find it easy to understand (because of the words in it) is the New International Version (NIV). I also appreciate The New King James version—one, because it is original from what I know, and two, because I can appreciate what came before the new and different or easier-to-understand versions. My dad told me always to pray for understanding before reading the Bible, I forget most of the time to pray before. Then there are times when I pray and do not ready my word; everything comes to understanding in God's timing. The important thing here to remember is to pray with faith, believing in what you are saying and asking of the Lord. The second thing to remember is to pray before reading your word while the third thing is to continue reading the Bible.

Say you are not religious or do not know Jesus Christ—then my advice for you is simply this: the things you do learn, whether in your profession, that of being a parent, a spouse, learning from your parents, I hope that you put it to good use in order to benefit yourselves, the ones you love, and for all those around you whether you think they are deserving or not.

Another way we learn to have a new attitude is through experiencing God's love. New can be different, and different can be new—sometimes we want new, and sometimes what we think is new is not. Sometimes it is just different, so it feels new and different. Therefore, what feels brand new is simply different than anything we have ever gone through before. Everyone wants new: new car, new house, new clothes, new day, or new year—just so we will not have to deal with the problems we face today. Being in the present moment will help you to stay on track. Paying attention to your five senses can help with staying in the moment, for those of you who have all of your five senses intact. Some people are robbed of their senses in life and others are born without them. When those who are born without any of their senses, or without more than one limb, then their other senses and parts of the body are heightened. They might have to rely on other parts of their body rather than if they were given these things. Say, when any of these five senses and or limbs are taken away from either ourselves (our own doing) because of certain choices, and or another person, or the enemy, then these people unfortunately/fortunately (depending how you look at it), will, may or may not look at life, themselves, and others around them differently. They might appreciate what they do or do not have, or they might take it all for granted.

Trying something new can be scary at first, but go for it anyway. When it is a good risk, the risk is always worth taking—especially if you have nothing to lose in the first place. Look at it this way: if it works out, then you will have gained; if it does not work out, then it was not meant to be. Your spirits may be let down, but this can be an opportunity to think about what you truly want in life. God will get to work on your heart and tell you exactly what it is he wants for you in your precious life.

The way that we think about thoughts and ideas that enter our head should be done with God in mind. But because we are human, we have thoughts that are not of God, thoughts that are either of ourselves from our own sinful nature, or thoughts that are evil. The thing is to *not* act on those evil thoughts. We could get an evil thought and it can grow with time, leading to more disgusting feelings, or we could grab and take hold of that evil thought and redirect it to a good thought.

Having the drive, the will power and the power of God working within us, determination not motivation because you won't always feel motivated, but discipline to help you accomplish and complete all that you want to get done and what God wants you to achieve. Motivation won't help because you won't always feel motivated to do Gods work. This is when prayer comes into play. Most importantly, have a good attitude. No one wants to have a bad attitude, even when it might seem more convincing in the moment to stay angry or upset about things and or people we can't change. We can, however, make a change starting with our own minds—people can only change themselves if they are willing to.

Say positive affirmations to yourself daily. In the morning, write things down that encourage and lift yourself up, such as special quotes, verses, and prayers. You can stick these on a sticky note or write them down on a notecard. The words and affirmations written down as a reminder are there to help you remember who God is and who you are in Christ.

When making choices, make them based on if it will please or displease the Lord. 1 Corinthians 3:16-17 says, "Don't you know that you yourselves are God's temple and that God's Spirit dwells in your midst? If anyone destroys God's temple, God will destroy that person; for God's temple is sacred, and you together are that temple." Be careful what you put into your body. 1 Corinthians 6:19-20 tells us: "Do you not know that your bodies are temples of the Holy Spirit, who is in you, whom you have received from God? You are not your own; you were bought at a price. Therefore honor God with your bodies." Respect yourselves, your body and those around you.

Change starts in your mind then shows in your actions. You can think about anything you want; you have the freedom and control of your innermost thoughts. Control your thoughts that lead to do better and want good, this will result in wanting a change and making a difference.

Use kind words with yourself. Don't beat yourself up, especially if you know deep down in your heart that you are trying and trusting God. In Psalms 141:3 says, "Set a guard over my mouth, LORD; keep watch over the door of my lips." Sometimes God puts words on a person's heart to say to another person, because the Lord knows they needed to hear it.

CHAPTER 6
DIFFERENT FOR EVERYONE

Just one more...one more piece, one more hit, one more drink—one more, one more quarter or dollar in the slot machine, one more steal or heist, one more lie, another deceit, another low blow, another past due payment, a new late fee, an eviction notice, not enough money, not enough sex. Not everyone has an addiction, so this part is for those who do, no matter what the addiction is. For those who don't have an addiction or unaware of one if any, proceed with caution—you will get advice that if put to effective use could benefit those around you who do struggle whether with addiction or unhealthy habits. Again, resisting temptation, as I mentioned in chapter four, is critical. Stay sober longer this time than last time. Begin by debating if you should do what you know you're not supposed to because you know it is bad for your health and not good for your relationships.

A.A.—Alcoholics Anonymous—works for some, helping them recover from their alcohol addiction. Some still fight the battle to want to drink daily—that is temptation that the enemy will use to keep us away from the Lord. I have an uncle who went to classes for years and is now a sponsor for those in need. One person once told me they weren't ready to quit. When and if you aren't ready to stop your bad habit, you will need support from family and friends, other resources, and God. Leaning on and relying on him is important in your recovery.

When making a goal, such as weight loss or gain, make it realistic and one that works for you. Remember what works for you may not work for the next person. Psalm 139:14 says, "I praise you because I am fearfully and wonderfully made; your works are wonderful, I know that full well." Take little steps to reach that goal, eating in moderation. Do not deprive yourself the healthy nutritious food your body craves. Appreciate your God given body—work to keep it healthy.

We all come in different shapes and sizes, no matter how small, tall, skinny, or heavy. When you look in the mirror after a workout, who are you seeking approval from? Is it for yourself, your partner, or the approval of others? Or is it for the honor, power, and glory that belongs to God? 1 Corinthians 10:31 says, "So whether you eat or drink or whatever you do, do it all for the glory of God."

Take that yoga class or boxing class you see and pass every day on your way to work. You may meet your future spouse without even knowing, just for being brave enough to try something you have always wanted to do. Joining a swim meet is a good workout for the whole entire body. A book club may be for you, if you enjoy discussing books, rather than writing them. Challenging yourself leads to great outcomes.

Poverty, low income, or come from little? Is it a challenge to pay your bills on time? Being dependent on the system—government help, support, or resources—it can be difficult to keep up with renewals, important dates, kid's school activities, or doctor's appointments. Even showing up to work can be an issue for some. Punctuality is necessary and required for most companies and businesses. Trying to accomplish routine tasks in our life may need little reminders here and there, such as a list written down of things to do on paper or in your phone. Support through family and friends is always helpful—when they do come through for us, be grateful and appreciative.

If you're in the military, is it challenging, difficult, and faith testing, to wake up early, to remind yourself why you are fighting for your country? You can execute tasks in frustration or tiredness, or you can choose to be of service and with love willingly continue to serve and to protect. Whatever God has given you, give it all you've got and use it when necessary. If you are a partner of someone in the military, be patient when it comes to waiting for your person to come home to you. Surprise them with more than just money bought gifts—surprise them with the best gift of all: your love. More importantly, show them Gods' love, because his is the best love. Love is something money can't buy—it is a free gift from the Lord. Cherish it and enjoy the love that is shared between two people that God brought together. Will you accept the Lord's free gift and his never-ending love?

It can be challenging to wake up, enraged and feeling helpless, having to rely on another in a lifeless situation. If and when you feel lifeless, useless, worthless any negative thought or feeling that may arise unexpectedly or purposely, just know that it is a lie—a big fat huge lie. Do not believe the negative thoughts in your mind; do not feed your head with doubt and fear—that is what the enemy wants, do not feed into this. Feed yourself with God's word, his truth, and his promises. I promise what God says about you is more important than what the enemy tries to convince you of or tries to convince you that you are *not*. Do not fall for his sweet persuasions—it is only a trick because he is a trickster.

The real battle is not on the battlefield—when you battle inside your mind that is when the real war comes. You then prepare yourself for the unthinkable. You might have your life flash before your eyes, and the good Lord might put on your heart to reflect on all that there is to be profoundly grateful for. This battle is not just a battle the men and women in service face—we as humans face a daily battle and how we choose to deal with it is entirely up to us. The battle we may face or choose to face is our own spirit; they could be that of our own selfish desires and that of the flesh.

Do you ever hear a voice in your head that says you are not good enough to do or be something, especially once God has called you to do something with your life, no matter what that something is? If so, ignore it, too. You are worthy—your worth is found in Christ alone. Let what God says be the deciding factor in what you do with your life. Of course, he gives us the freedom to choose. The thing is, God wants and hopes that you choose him over every other thing in this world first. Putting him first above every other evil selfish thing in our hearts and our minds will ensure that you lead a fulfilling life in Christ and his works.

Instead of saying "one more, just one more," trust me I know, I have said this to myself quietly inside my head, thinking I am done, because my mind tells me I am done, but my inner defiance say to me, "you'll be fine, go ahead, one more, you should be okay), say "No more!" Even if it is just one more hit, say no to that *one* more hit so that you do *not* overdo it. Know your limits, and if you're unsure you will find out soon enough. God has given us food to enjoy; he has given us just what we need and recognizing this is key. Sin can be enticing.

PERSONAL GROWTH

As humans, beyond an addiction or curiosity, we need to be able to say no. Have enough self-discipline and self-control to say *no* to that one more hit. Then and only then will you realize that it will soon get easier to continue to say no to the things that no longer serve its purpose in your life. Believe that even the bad choices in our lives have a purpose—we have to take the good with the bad, and God always takes the bad and turns it into good. Remember that nothing can happen without the Lord's permission—nothing, and no one is hidden from God's sight. He sees what happens when the doors are open and he sees what is behind closed doors. So even when we try to hide, know that there is no hiding from God—his presence is omniscient.

What growth looks like for one person may look like something totally different for someone else. Don't give up—don't stop trying even when it seems impossible. What is impossible for man, is possible for God, if it is in his will. Take a break, get some rest, and walk away for a minute, but do not quit. Put in the work, no matter what. Go the extra mile if you need to and do not be afraid of starting over. As long as there is progression happening, you will keep moving forward.

To make progress might mean taking baby steps; it might mean giving up something that is hard to give up; it might mean changing your eating habits; it might mean lowering your voice to make those around you less nervous. In the same way a parent might get frustrated when their child does no listen when told to do something we've asked of them-God rebukes us, corrects us, and disciplines us when we don't listen. He does this in a loving manner, of course—not for punishment but in order to learn; not be condemned or feel bad about a mistake, but in hopes that we will choose not to make the same mistake.

The challenges you might face such as temptation, fear, worry, or doubt, can lead us to live in fear. Who wants to be afraid all the time? Well, you do not have to be—learning to let go of these doubts is crucial.

We as humans are not to be judged by ourselves or others; the true judgment is rightfully God's and belongs to him. Mathew 7:1 says, "Do not judge, or you too will be judged." It takes time to adjust, grow, and mature in Christ—physically, mentally, and emotionally. To grow your spirit takes practice, like reading your word every day, even if it is just one verse a day. To grow in your spirit takes time, through meditation, faith, and patience, you will grow to understand all you can ask Christ for in his name. To grow emotionally means to be able to manage and control your emotions in a way that will not harm yourself or others. To grow mentally, feed your mind with God's word, good thoughts, and knowledge that you can later use to help those in need. To grow physically would include eating healthily, by having a well-balanced nutritional diet that works for you.

Food that is and might be good, healthy, strengthening, helpful and nutritional to one person might not be to another, for specific reasons. Such as sugar and or salt, remember that too much of anything is not good for you. In Proverbs 25:16, it says, "If you find honey, eat just enough-too much of it, and you will vomit." Too much sugar can cause cavities; too much salt can cause strokes, heart disease, or water retention. My son ate too many Nerds candy one day without my permission. He later started throwing up. When he was done throwing up, he admitted to me that he ate the rest of the candy after I told him not to. With a saddened look on his face, his chin down to his chest. I'll never forget that moment. In the same way, the good Lord might tell his children not to do something that will end up hurting us or making us sick, yet we sometimes do it anyway and regret it later. We pay for it and suffer for our poor choices and disobedience.

Finding a workout regimen that works for you and your body type is beneficial, since everyone's bodies are shaped differently. Changing any bad eating habits now will benefit you in your later age if you want to age gracefully. Remember that everything is best in moderation, leading to a healthy life.

The change and difference you see in yourself and in others is going to look, feel, and be different than the next person. Your pace may be different, slower, or faster depending on the plans God has for your life.

Trust God's plans rather than your own—his are far better and greater than what we could ever plan.

CHAPTER 7
SOMETIMES MANDATORY

Our own personal choices force us to grow; we must change and do things differently in our lives to see different results. Pushed by God and the Holy Spirit in a safe way can redirect and help us. God protects us from the evil that we cannot always see with the naked eye because sometimes we are blinded. Sometimes God or our personal choices will put us in a position where we may have no choice but to learn and grow from a situation or be lost and drown. The choice is ours though, and God gives us the freedom to choose. This can be scary, but God says, in Isaiah 41:10, "So do not fear, for I am with you; do not be dismayed, for I am your God." Sometimes God will leave us with no other choice but to lean on him and cry out to him with what is bothering us or standing in our way. When we do this, he helps us out in unsurmountable ways that only God himself can explain. He will show you this in ways only you can understand. When he does this, this is him talking to you and guiding you through the Holy Spirit—his peace will be with you. He says in Isaiah 26:12: "Lord, you establish peace for us; all that we have accomplished you have done for us." You will feel calm and at ease; the pressures and weight of the world on your shoulders will be lifted.

When standing in our own way—which as humans we tend to do without thought—can cause us to delay or hinder our progress, growth, success, health, and spiritual growth. If you do stumble and are standing in your own way, do not worry, because you can just as easily get out of your own way. When you fall back, it just means you need to better prepare for the next time.. Try to prevent there being a next time—do not let yourself hold yourself back any longer.

Personal growth is sometimes mandatory if we want to see the change in ourselves that we are so afraid to see. Knowing how great we can truly be—with God's help—keeps us on track. When we allow fear to creep it, we are not doing what God has called us to do. If you are going to fear anything, fear God out of respect. Isaiah 41:13 says, "For I am the LORD your God who takes hold of your right hand and says to you, Do not fear; I will help you." Do not let fear keep you from giving something you know you are good at, all your efforts to do the work of God. Whatever it is the good Lord has called you to do, do it mightily and with heart. Ephesians 6:7 says, "Serve wholeheartedly, as if you were serving the Lord, not people." Whether it be the garbage man who uses God's strength to help him lift the trash can to the garbage truck, or if it's the CEO of a booming business, the knowledge comes from the Lord. A teacher who is a true disciple of the Lord has a great amount of influence on the children in their classroom, use that time to your advantage to help others get to God's kingdom and closer to Christ. Do not be afraid.

At times we need a little encouragement through words, action, disappointment, or mistakes made from self and others, in order to get to the next step in our lives and to where we need to be. This helps us serve a higher purpose other than ourselves.

Do you ever feel stuck? What is holding you back? What is keeping you from doing what God has called you to do? Sometimes stagnation is a good thing. This waiting period—even though it can feel useless or tiresome—can be a period of not only growth but self-improvement.

One more haircut, ladies, c'mon. You can do it, right before you take your thirty-minute lunch break. Every once in a while, cover for someone's shift; you never know how much they really needed that shift covered. Stay an extra haircut or two later (which, depending on your cut time and the service(s) being provided, is no more than an hour extra, tops). A sense of urgency shows your clients that you care. Nurses, I know you work that four-on, three-off and cover and take on more hours—because you need it for bills, or your children, and other reasons of course, like compassion, or because no one else will cover their shift and you're the only one left to do it. Men and women in the service, one more day, one more month, you are so close to being home with your spouse/family/loved ones and friends. For those at home waiting for your family member to return back safely in one piece, keep them covered in prayer. You never know what your faith in believing what God can do or will protect your loved one from. Letting go is being able to move forward. Let go of the past and all the things that are not good for you or no longer serve a purpose in your life for the better.

To grow, do or try something different; take notes or note it in your head if what you did differently worked or not. Even if we do not want to or feel like making the changes necessary to grow, sometimes it is needed for a new door to open.

God will use whoever whenever and however he pleases—no questions asked. He will do this without hesitation so that his purpose is fulfilled for his glory. Isaiah 14:24 says, "The LORD Almighty has sworn, "Surely, as I have planned, so it will be, and as I have purposed, so it will happen." When it is mandatory, we really have no choice in the matter about what God says to us.

CHAPTER 8
TAKES ENCOURAGEMENT

Personal growth requires encouraging words from ourselves and others who are important to us. God encourages us to keep our hope in him. Through his word, he encourages us and lifts us up, helping us through our difficulties even when we do not see it. The Lord is our help and support.

He encourages us to follow his instructions and commandments in Exodus 20:1–17. These were given to Moses as a reminder of what God has called us to do. Let's be faithful and obedient servants of Christ.

Most importantly, treat others how you want to be treated, my mother used to remind me and my siblings, just like in Mathew 7:12 says, "So in everything, do to others what you would have them do to you, for this sums up the law and the Prophets." God's commandment says to love your neighbor as you love yourself, only acting toward others as you would have them act with you—therefore, if there was something you never want done to you, do not do it yourself. If we cannot do something ourselves, how can we possibly ask or expect someone else to do what it is we are asking them to do, whether good or bad?

Let's look at an example of this. A mother and her child walk into a grocery store. As the two of them walk down an aisle, they run into another cart, accidentally knocking off some of the overfilled groceries. The customer with the knocked off groceries did not see this happen, as they were reading a label on a food item. The child continued to push their cart in the opposite direction of the knocked over groceries, not saying and or doing anything about it. The mother realized that the other person's groceries were on the ground. She looked over at her child and asked, "Did you accidentally hit their cart?"

"Maybe," the child replied.

"Well, c'mon—let's help them pick these up since we knocked them over." The child was embarrassed and thought the person would not notice the knocked over groceries. "How would you feel if someone else accidentally ran into us and did what you did then not help, pretending they did not know what happened?" the mother asked. She continued, "It would not be very nice now, would it?"

"No," the child replied. Paying attention and being self-aware of yourself and your surroundings can and will prevent accidents from happening.

We are not always mindful or consideration of people and their thoughts and feelings as humans. Titus 3:2 says, "to slander no one, to be peaceable and considerate, and always to be gentle toward everyone." This translates to put others before yourself. Philippians 2:3-4 "Do nothing out of selfish ambition or vain conceit. Rather, in humility value others before yourselves, not looking to your own interests but each of you to the interests of the others." Of course, there are times when being kind or practicing generosity cannot happen. In those moments, God is possibly teaching someone a lesson, such as a moment of waiting and being patient.

Joshua 1:9 says, "Have I not commanded you? Be strong and courageous. Do not be afraid; do not be discouraged, for the LORD your God will be with you wherever you go." You don't have to feel alone but when you do, know that the Lord is right there with you through it all. 1 Thessalonians 5:11 says, "Therefore encourage one another and build each other up, just as in fact you are doing." Keep building each other up with kind words; keep serving the Lord in all that you do—God encourages this.

Being brave and doing something that takes major courage will not always be the easiest. Take risks, take chances, and choose wisely. If you were not so afraid of anything, then there would be nothing to fight for. Gear your fear toward your greatest aspirations. We can use self-affirmations—quotes, scripture, etc.—which can lead to reassurance.

Whatever you choose, at times you may fail and fall. When you do, get right back up—or don't—the choice is yours. You can deal with, react, or respond to how and when you fall however you want..

Personal growth sometimes means letting go—letting go of the old and the past so you're able to bring in the new. This allows you to look forward to the future and all that God has in store for you and your loved ones. Romans 12:2 says, "Do not conform to the pattern of this world, but be transformed by the renewing of your mind. Then you will be able to test and approve what God's will is—his good, pleasing and perfect will." 2 Corinthians 5:17 says, "Therefore, if anyone is in Christ, the new creation has come: The old has gone, the new is here!" Invite the new—welcome the bright beginnings that lay ahead and look forward to all you can accomplish with the Lord's help.

Celebrate your newly innovative ideas without fear about what others will say. Celebrate your little achievements—and the big ones, too. Never stop hoping to be better and to achieve greater than what you did before. Do not fear—failure and success go hand in hand. Remember to dream huge. If that dream was put in your heart and will not go away, I suggest doing something about it. God holds the future and all the possibilities that might come your way in his hands. Remember that with God, all things are possible—without him, everything in life is mediocre. A life with Christ might seem or appear to be boring to some, but routine and mundane daily duties as a Christian is more rewarding than choosing a life of sin. Celebrate how hard you have worked and how far you have come—whether you see it or know it, you were being encouraged and led by the Holy Spirit. He was guiding you and your heart through what you were dealing with at the time of affliction, regret, remorse, guilt, shame, anger, or sadness. He has always been there to help and support you on your journey in this beautiful thing we call life.

Continue to strive to be better by encouraging yourself and lifting others up as you continue to walk this earth—leave patterns that are untraceable. Never deny what the good Lord can and would do for you, because in his timing what you ask for you shall receive. God's word says: "Ask and it will be given to you; seek and you will find; knock and the door will be opened to you. For everyone who asks receives; the one who seeks finds; and to the one who knocks, the door will be opened." (Mathew 7:7-8). Love someone in a way that when others see the love you have for them, it is undeniable. Hopefully, they can and will see the good Lord's undeniable love. If you are going to rely on anyone or anything, let it be the Lord, for he is our one true undeniable and reliable resource. If you hope for anything, let it be hope in the Lord, for he is good. Hebrews 11:1 says, "Now faith in confidence in what we hope for and assurance about what we don't see." Hope for good and do good, remembering that what is good in man's eyes may not be good in God's eyes. 1 Samuel 16:7 says, "But the Lord said to Samuel, 'Do not consider his appearance or his height, for I have rejected him. The Lord does not look at the things people look at. People look at the outward appearance, but the Lord looks at the heart.'"

If you do trust in anyone, let it be the Lord. If you do not trust in anyone or anything, then my dear friend, you have already lost hope, and for that I hope and pray that you will find it again Your faith will be evaluated, like going through the fire—after you will be like gold, refined and ready to be presented to Christ. Isaiah 64:8 says "Yet you, LORD, are our Father. We are the clay, you are the potter; we are all the work of your hand." Temptations never go away even though the devil will flee when you pray. It is the not acting on any of the temptations to focus on, which is and can be the hard part. Once tested and choosing right, the victory will be yours and the Lord's to celebrate forever. Now that is a win-win situation—what a delight to be in the presence of the Lord.

What is right to one man may not be right to another, so choose what is wise in God's eyes. His wisdom, will guide you and help you through your difficulties and the next steps in your life. When you decide to lean on him, trust him and go to him with every single detail and account of your life. If something is bothering you, tell Jesus about it; if you are worried, scared, or stressed, talk to Jesus about it. He is a wonderful listener. There have been plenty of times when I needed or wanted someone, anyone to listen to me—to hear what I had to say even if it was ridiculous sounding. When I didn't have that or when I thought that no one would understand me, I had Jesus to turn to, look to, pray to, talk to, cry to, scream to, and yell to. He always listens.

You will not always be encouraged or feel encouraged to do what is right. I encourage you to keep going. Rest when needed; stop and do not go any further if warned through people, places, your intuition, or through the Holy Spirit. Learning to release and let go of anything that does not serve your soul's purpose in life is bravery—it takes great courage and will benefit you. Your personal growth does not always look like how you want or expect it to—sometimes your personal growth turns out to be even better. It can be and will be painful at times, but it is oh so worth it. Keep fighting the good fight and persevere.

MY PERSONAL THANK YOU

My personal thank you to a man named Mathew, who is oh so kind, patient, and understanding—a few of the quality characteristic traits that the Lord possesses. Thank you for showing up after having to reschedule due to previous engagements, as well as for understanding that appointments can going over the time allotted. You have done a service not only to me, but to the Lord and his kingdom. You will be rewarded—continue to do good works, for the Lord sees you. Psalms 128:2 states, "You will eat the fruit of your labor; blessings and prosperity will be yours." If it weren't for your help and assistance along with God, this beautiful and wonderful start of mine would not have happened. Thank you again—I am grateful and appreciative of your time and the arduous work you put in to not please me, but to please the Lord.

    Thank you so much to my publisher's Troy Palmetto, my project manager Chole Tunis, my editors Beth and

Kirstin; as well as my cover design team and all who helped with making this a reality. You will forever be remembered.

A very personal thank you to Christ Jesus, without you none of this would be happening. You are my greatest counselor and my greatest hero. You are my comfort always and my joy after mourning. You are my go-to when I need a listening ear, who is oh so understanding, forgiving, and more than kind. You, Lord, get all my thanks. Thanks be to God. 2 Corinthians 9:15 implies this: "Thanks be to God for his indescribable gift." I am grateful Lord, knowing that everything has come from you. Ephesians 5:20 says, "always thanks to God the Father for everything in the name of our Lord Jesus Christ."

Thank you for picking this book up and taking time to comprehend and understand what it is the good Lord wants you to. Never stop aiming for personal growth; continue to seek spiritual growth for our personal relationship with Jesus Christ is a lifetime opportunity that is never ending.

Now get you something to celebrate your personal growth with—a delicious cupcake or flowers for yourself or your loved one to celebrate yours, his, or her "Personal Growth." Remembering and keep in mind that this does not happen overnight. You did an excellent job in finishing this book in the time you did—all your hard work will pay off as long as you stay consistent with what you aim for. Encourage others to do the same by lending this book to a friend or family member that needs assistance or a push in their journey to personal growth.

WORKS CITED-REFERENCES

Scripture taken from the HOLY BIBLE, NEW INTERNATIONAL VERSION NIV. Copyright 1973, 1978, 1984, 2011 by Biblica, Inc. Used by permission of Biblica, Inc. All rights reserved worldwide.

Quoted Scripture NIV

FOLLOW ME!

@ISTAY_SWEET_PEBBLELICIOUS

https://www.facebook.com/Pebbles-Hopke

ABOUT THE AUTHOR

A writer since she was eight years old, Pebbles Hopke has dreamt of publishing a book for years. After publishing Personal Growth, she expects many more to come.

Born and raised amid the beautiful, colorful, and unpredictable weather of Colorado Springs, Pebbles still calls the Centennial State home. She enjoys spending time with family.

Most of the time, you can find Pebbles somewhere in nature with her family, listening to aspiring music at home, dancing for fun, scrapbooking, creating fun-filled memories, or reading and writing.

www.ingramcontent.com/pod-product-compliance
Lightning Source LLC
LaVergne TN
LVHW012036060526
838201LV00061B/4633